SINTEXT

By Mihika Menezes

Author's Note

I began writing as a way to shed the darkness within me. This collection has been an intensely personal journey. While I faced moments of doubt and hardships, wishing to give up on life, I realized that writing these poems gave me a blanket full of warmth that covered my pain and made me stronger.

I decided to compile this collection of poetry that I have been writing since 2017. A brilliant thought, if I do say so myself! My brain, affectionately named Ashmika, has truly been my greatest ally in navigating the highs and lows of creativity.

We often give ourselves little credit for our accomplishments, so here's to my work reflecting the perseverance that has carried me through each challenge. It's a reminder that even in my darkest moments, I could create something meaningful.

I want to thank myself for pushing through, for surviving, and for bringing this poetry to life. My journey has often felt solitary, so I owe it to myself.

These days, I am learning to accept myself and be kinder to myself. It's a tough journey, but I'm making progress. So, thank you to me and my beautiful mind for conjuring these lovely words!

With gratitude filling my heart, I would also like to acknowledge the support systems around me, such as my great family, my loving and supportive partner and his family, my therapist, all the nuns that believed in my potential, my dearest professor's who never gave up on me, my support group, and my lovely friends.

I celebrate my courage for enduring, my mind (Ashmika!) for its resilience, and my heart for its refusal to give up.

This collection is my silent strength, put into words. Lastly, thank YOU! for taking the time to read my poems. You have been a wonderful reader. Happy Reading!

CONTENTS

A Letter to My Child—By *Life*

Child, was it not easy to be the
best among all, as well as honest
every time?
Do not tell me that I didn't give
you a chance to decide.
I know it was not easy to kill your
emotions and your feelings
For someone whom you once
loved, you cared for, and called
"mine."

I always knew it was not easy, not
even an inch, to say "Goodbye."
But darling, I did give you a
choice.

I knew it was not easy for you to
have the best of friends,
which you then called "thine."

Here again, I tried to stop you, but
you never listened.
As you thought they were your
best friends, always right,
and all that they did was just fine.

I knew it well; it wasn't easy to
walk away when you had tears
rolling down your eyes.
But my love, I beckoned you
through that one person to stop by
and think again,
which you refused back then to do,
as you thought you were all right.

Yes, I know it was never easy when
you knew the truth,
but you still had to sit there and
just sigh.
As I knew back then, it was again

your mistake;
you had a choice.
You chose the wrong person—not
once, but twice.

Was it that easy when someone
looked you in the eye,
spoke to you with confidence, and
you knew all that was discussed
was just a lie?
But again, I would blame you,
as you left them with no other
reason than to lie.

I knew, my child, it was not easy to
look up at the Almighty
and ask for forgiveness, even when
you knew you couldn't forgive
yourself,
and all you wanted to do was give

up on me—that was your life.
As for now, even I knew your heart
could no longer keep up
with the pain, loathe, or strife.

You may be wondering by now,
Was I ever easy on you?
Think again, my beloved; I
would now just want to look up
at you
with my graceful smile.
For some humans, I agree;
they say maybe I wasn't tough
on them,
but I would like to mention it
was always a matter of fact
that I did give you a choice
between what's right and
what's not right.

A choice to choose between the best and the worst for you, which you, my love, foolishly kept wasting and then cried.

They did tell you to keep me simple, take me as I come, and do not hurt others.
I do remember them warning you about my friend Karma, who would then come back to you,
having a look upon your deeds, and deciding whether to twinkle you with showers of blessings or dress you in garments full of curses.
My message is to convey my thoughts to you

so that you know that I can no
longer deal with your lies,
but I will still try.

But right now,
I would want to look into your
eyes with the stern, hysterical
look
that I always had when I
looked at you
and ask you just that one
question for the last time.
Are you still persistent enough
to continue along with your
sins?
Or is it too early to ask you by
now?
Should we maintain our
distance?

As we can no longer get along
with your sinful mistakes
that you keep denying, you
keep denying,
and pushing it all on me,
while you kept saying,
It was all your mistake and not
mine?

A New Sunset

With every new sunset,
the sunrise had a little bet.
"I'm sure you won't be able to
make it till tomorrow," the sun
says.
"We shall see how long you
last, my dear sunrays."

With this childish attitude, they
never fail to please
us humans, who are always
racing with ease.
But one fine day, the sun
thought to itself,
"What if I don't rise? What if I
don't heed the hen's cries?"

But that's not how humans
would take my apology;
they would blame me for not
showing up,
They would blame me for not
wrapping up.

As the day faded, the sunset
glowed,
painting the sky in hues, a
magical road.
The stars twinkled softly,
whispering tales
of dreams and wishes riding
gentle gales.

"What if the night takes over
my throne?"
The sun pondered, feeling all
alone.

Yet the moon, with its silver beams so bright,
promised to guide through the peaceful night.

And so, with all those thoughts in mind,
the sun was reminded of the little bet made that night.
Just like that, it showed up with a beautiful and bright light.

Restless

My eyelids feel heavy as I
begin to lay down.
I think of that beautiful day in
town.
But everything's blurry, even
the tiniest bit of memory.
I guess it was only because I
had been trying to erase those
thoughts, not so cleverly.

I try my level best to sleep each
time I shut my eyes,
but my mind keeps thinking of
being awake while it
apologizes.
Maybe it's time to let go of
those blurry memories.

At least it will let my mind come in peace with my enemies.

But again, can memories be erased?
Maybe not, but with time, they could definitely be misplaced.
You may be wondering why a beautiful day would want to be erased so badly.
Well, sometimes, darling, even beautiful things can make you sad.

The laughter, the joy, and the warmth of the sun
now feel like shadows of the battles I've run.
Each smile shared was a

double-edged sword,
reminding me of moments I
can't quite afford.

And so, even the vague thought
of those memories
disappearing gives me peace
of mind.
It shuts my mind and makes it
blind.
Yet I ponder the price of this
quiet retreat.
Am I losing the beauty, or is it
just bittersweet?

If memories fade, will I still
know their grace?
Will I lose the feelings that
time cannot replace?
So I lie here in the silence,

wrestling with my heart,
wanting to let go but afraid to part.

Perhaps it's in acceptance that healing begins,
embracing both joy and the ache that it brings.
So, as I drift off, I'll carry them near,
for the beauty in pain is what keeps me here.

You Need You!

Don't run after something that
doesn't want you, child;
it's definitely the wrong
number that you have dialed.
Darling, know your worth,
as you've turned out to be
beautiful from the time of your
birth.

You may think this person is
everything you wished for,
but have you been paying
attention to the signs that you
ignore?
These instincts that are telling
you to step away
Are you mistaken by whispers

from your heart urging you to stay?

When you look back and think about it, sweetheart,
it won't matter to you; it will be just a tiny part.
A tiny part of your life, as beautiful and painful as art,
but it helped you grow, keeping everything apart.

You've changed now for the better good.
It's something that happened over time, as you understood.
Just keep reminding yourself that you are stronger than you think, and everything will fall into place within a blink.

Yes, sometimes your days will
be tough and rough,
but remember all the things
that helped you grow tough.
All you need is you in the end,
my love,
for your soul is beautiful and
pure, like that of a dove.

Embrace the journey, with all
its twists and turns,
for each experience is a
lesson; each moment, it
yearns.
You are a masterpiece,
evolving each day.
So cherish your spirit and let
nothing sway.

Choose You!

Choosing peace over anything
isn't a sign of weakness;
you're protecting yourself from
going near any kind of
darkness.

I'm sure it's tough to walk
away from those you once had
a deep connection with.
But, darling, your sanity is
much more valuable to begin
with.

They say you rise each time
you fall,
but always remember, your
smallest efforts count, after all.

Nothing stays forever.
So, darling, choose yourself,

choose yourself,

I'm sure you're that clever!

Freedom

I met this stranger with
beautiful eyes.
We got into talking, and it felt
so nice.
While getting to know each
other,
they asked me, "Who are you?"
I wasn't very sure, so I paused
for a while.

I asked them who they were,
to which they replied,
"I am love, I am care,
I am freedom; this is how I
define."

That's when I realized
and spoke it out loud for the

first time:
"I think I am freedom,
as I need to express myself in
my kingdom."

To which they said, "You're a
wonderful person, one of a
kind.
Someone who wishes to help
others,
who finds joy in doing that in
their mind."

Now that I think about it,
Yes, I believe that's where I
shine.
Helping others gives me peace
and gives me immense joy.
Knowing new faces gives me

that thrill.
It makes me feel like I enjoy it.

I enjoy my time around new
faces;
I enjoyed my time when I heard
that beautiful new voice—that
voice that spoke to me that
day—about their career and
their passion,
with a lot of love, glee,
serenity,
and bliss in their twinkling eye.

I wish to explore such
wonderful, different souls
Now and then,
As that adrenaline rush that I
receive
Makes me feel like,

"This is my life! This is my fashion!
This is my style!"

Mistakes

Why don't I let myself make
mistakes?
While typing, I easily delete
the errors that I create.
Then why, Lord, why don't I let
myself make mistakes?

I pressurize myself to be the
best at everything I can,
but that always lets me down
in all my plans.
Sometimes I wish that I could
see the picture from afar—the
journey of growth, my own
guiding star.

I see others stumble and rise
with grace,

learning and growing at their own pace.
Why do I hold myself to a standard so high
when the beauty of life lies in the lows and the highs?

Mistakes are just lessons, steps in disguise,
leading me closer to my own true prize.
Yet, fear clings tightly, whispering in my ear,
telling me failure is something to fear.

But now I realize, as I reflect on my scars,
that each misstep is a compass, guiding me to who we are.

Instead of letting shame dictate
how far I can go,
I'll embrace each mistake as
part of my growth.

As everyone makes mistakes, I
understand with clarity:
They don't define me; they're a
part of my journey.
So I'll shed the weight of
perfection I wore
and open my heart to learn
and explore.

The Voice Inside Me

The voice inside me keeps
questioning, "Are you fine?"
Whenever I am sad, it makes
me feel dead inside.
I wonder if it truly helps me
shine
Or if it deepens the wounds, I
try to hide.

The voice knows what's right;
it never leaves my side.
I'm writing this sad poem after
ages.
It's borne from my struggles,
the storms I can't abide,
fighting the rages that fill these
pages.

The voice inside me wants to scream,
It's known for too long what's wrong and what's right.
But mostly, it finds comfort in a dream,
And hides in the shadows, avoiding the light.

"I want to be free," says the voice inside of me.
But I am too scared to let it fly, too scared to break free from this misery,
afraid of the truth that I can't deny.

Yet, I know there's a fire yearning to ignite—a longing for truth, for clarity, for light.

If I could gather the courage to
face what I fear,
perhaps I'd find strength in the
whispers I hear.

So I'll sit with this voice, let it
speak loud and clear,
and in the silence of my heart,
I'll learn to be free.
To embrace all the chaos, to
draw it near,
and finally understand the
voice within me.

Silent Strength Spoken By Words

It feels so alone, do you know
why?
The alphabet won't join to
form a word.
Not a single letter will even
try;
It's as if words have gone
unheard.

Alphabets scatter, happy and
free,
Not caring for the words they
leave behind.
In their own worlds, they'd
rather be;
To a word's plea, they stay
blind.

Words were always there to
give them a place,
But now the letters don't seem
to care.
Words cry out, but it's all in
vain;
The letters move on, unaware.

Words beg and plead for them
to unite,
But excuses keep the letters
away.
Yet words won't fade or lose
their fight;
They'll find new ways, come
what may.

For words are strong; they will
endure,
Even if letters refuse to stay.

They'll rise again, of that, they're sure,
And stand tall in their own way.

SINTEXT

I chose the word "Sintext" for
the way it connects,

The power of words to heal or
reflect.

A careless word can create a
sin.

But the right one can spark the
light within.

Each word we choose holds a
space,

In someone's heart, their
world, their place.

Sinful words can shatter and
bind.

While gentle ones leave warmth behind.

So, dear readers, choose with care,

Let kindness guide the words you share.

Sintext is a reminder, a truth profound,

That the words we speak shape the world around.

www.ingramcontent.com/pod-product-compliance
Lightning Source LLC
LaVergne TN
LVHW041301150826
845673LV00008B/2685
* 9 7 9 8 8 9 0 6 7 5 0 6 4 *